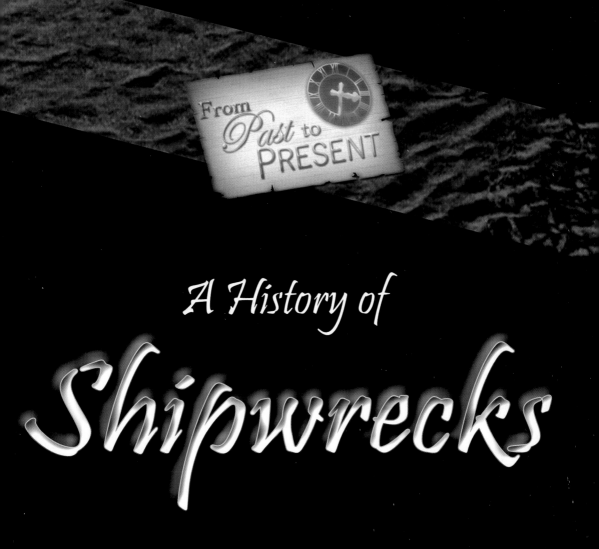

From
Past to
PRESENT

A History of

Shipwrecks

by David and Susan Spence

GARETH**STEVENS**
GS
PUBLISHING
A Member of the WRC Media Family of Companies

Please visit our web site at: **www.garethstevens.com**
For a free color catalog describing Gareth Stevens Publishing's list of high-quality books
and multimedia programs, call 1-800-542-2595 (USA) or 1-800-387-3178 (Canada).
Gareth Stevens Publishing's fax: (414) 332-3567.

Library of Congress Cataloging-in-Publication Data

Spence, David, 1957-
    A history of shipwrecks / David and Susan Spence. — North American ed.
        p. cm. — (From past to present)
    Includes index.
    ISBN 0-8368-6288-0 (lib. bdg.)
    1. Shipwrecks—Juvenile literature. I. Spence, Susan. II. Title. III. Series.
    G525.S626   2006
    910.4'52—dc22   2005054082

This North American edition first published in 2006 by
Gareth Stevens Publishing
A Member of the WRC Media Family of Companies
330 West Olive Street, Suite 100
Milwaukee, WI 53212 USA

This edition copyright © 2006 by Gareth Stevens, Inc. Original edition copyright © 2003 by ticktock Entertainment Ltd. First published in
Great Britain in 1997 by ticktock Media Ltd., Unit 2, Orchard Business Centre, North Farm Road, Tunbridge Wells, Kent, TN2 3 XF.
Additional end matter copyright © 2006 by Gareth Stevens, Inc.

Gareth Stevens editor: Leifa Butrick
Gareth Stevens designer: Kami M. Strunsee

The publishers would like to thank Graham Rich, Rosalind Beckman and Elizabeth Wiggans for their assistance and David Hobbs for his map
of the world.

Picture Credits: t=top, b=bottom, c=center, l=left, r=right
AKG; IFC, 7c, 11t, 13t, 12cr, 14cr & 34c, 18c. Ann Ronan Picture Library; 4b, 4c, 4tr. Cephas Picture Library/Mick Rock; 16b. Chris Fairclough
Colour Library; 17c. Colorific; 5b, 10cl, 22t, 22b, 29t & 32cl. CORBIS; 26l, 27l, 26cr2, 26cr3, 26cr1, 27r & 32cr. Draeger Limited; 5c. e.t. archive;
14b, 20b. FPG International; 24c. Giraudon; 19b & 32cr. Glasgow Museums: The Stirling Maxwell Collection, Pollok House; 12cl. Hulton
Getty; 21c, 21t, 25c. Illustrated London News; 22c. Institute of Nautical Archaeology; 9t, 9b, 8c, 9c, 8b. John Eaton and Charles Haas; 21bl.
Mary Evans Picture Library; 15t, 24b, 25t, 25b. Mary Rose Trust; 10c, 11cr, 10b. National Maritime Museum; 12b, 15b & 32t, 16c, 17t, 17b, 19c,
32br, 23b. Planet Earth; OFC (diver), 5t, 6b, 14cl & 32bl. Rex Features; 7t, 28l, 29b, 29c, 28r, 31t, 31b, 31cl, 30c, 31cr. Spectrum Colour Library;
30b. Telegraph Colour Library; 6t, 6c, 11b. The Kobal Collection; 23c, 23t. The Stock Market; 7 (main pic). ticktock Entertainment Limited;
15c. Trustees of the National Museums and Galleries of Northern Ireland; 13bl, 13cr. Ulster Folk and Transport Museum; 20t. Utopia
Productions; 18b.

Printed in the United States of America

1 2 3 4 5 6 7 8 9 10 09 08 07 06

CONTENTS

Words that appear in the glossary are printed in
boldface type the first time they occur in the text.

Shipwrecks are as ancient as ships, and the treasures that divers haul from the hull of sunken ships bring us messages from the past. Some of the best evidence we have of ancient civilizations has come from wrecked ships. The wrecks are like **time capsules** because they give us valuable information about how ships were built, the crews that sailed them, and the passengers and cargoes they carried. This evidence helps researchers build a vivid picture of the society of the time. Today, sophisticated technology allows us to investigate deep beneath the waves, and **vessels** such as the *Titanic* are beginning to yield their secrets.

The Diving Barrel

Jacob Rowe's diving barrel, invented in 1753, was an early, if crude, piece of diving **apparatus**. The hollow copper vessel had a glass window at one end and two holes for the occupant's arms. The encased diver was lowered from a ship and could stay underwater until all the air inside had been used up. Often, the diver could stay below for thirty minutes.

The Diving Suit

C. H. Klingert invented a flexible diving suit in 1797. It was made of watertight leather and tinplate (thin sheets of steel coated with tin). The diver was free to walk around on the seabed. The ship above supplied air through tubes.

The Diving Bell

A man in a diving bell could submerge but breathe air through a tube to the surface. The principle has been known and tried since the time of Aristotle (350 B.C.). In the early eighteenth century, Edmund Halley produced a crude diving bell made of wood and coated with lead to make it heavy enough to sink. It was bell-shaped and had a top of clear glass to provide light. It also had a device to let out used-up air. The bell could go as deep as 60 feet (18 meters).

The Underwater Lung

Modern undersea exploration made much progress after 1943, when Jacques Yves Cousteau and Emile Gagnan invented the **aqualung**. The new diving apparatus adapted an air-regulating device that had been used in wartime, gas-driven car engines. Aqualungs automatically provide air to divers from bottles strapped to their backs. Divers are now free of the heavy diving gear they needed previously.

The Armored Suit

The deeper a diver goes, the greater the water pressure. The most modern diving suits, called **atmospheric diving suits**, are armored and able to withstand the incredible water pressure generated by the tons of water above a diver's head. The suit also maintains tolerable air pressure inside and allows divers to go as deep as 1,180 feet (360 m). The design is based on early suits of armor, with jointed arms and legs to permit freedom of movement.

Searching the Wrecks

Diving on wrecks is a popular pastime as well as a serious venture, and, with the aid of a **wet suit** and aqualung, diving enthusiasts around the world search for the treasures of the deep.

Ships face many dangers on open seas. Storms, fog, and underwater reefs are as dangerous as they ever were, although today's technology gives a vigilant crew more advanced warning than sailors used to have. Accurate weather forecasting and ship-to-shore communication mean that vessels are able to take evasive actions when storms approach, either by sheltering in harbors or by taking alternative routes. All seagoing ships now carry **global positioning systems (GPS)** that use satellite technology to fix their positions with pinpoint accuracy. Similarly advanced equipment determines how much clearance there is between a ship's **hull** and the seabed. Maps of the coastlines, detailed charts, and knowledgeable pilots help a ship's crew navigate successfully. The age-old hazards of the sea, however, remain.

Coral Reefs

Reefs are ridges of rock, sand, or coral that lie close to the surface of the sea. Ships risk running aground on these ridges, which can cause fatal damage to the hull or prevent a ship from moving. Hard coral reefs grow extremely slowly, so reefs damaged by ships may take hundreds of years to recover.

Icebergs

Icebergs are floating masses of frozen freshwater that have broken off an ice sheet. They are most common in spring when warm weather melts the ice shelves. Icebergs can be small lumps of ice or huge blocks the size of ten-story buildings. Only one-seventh is visible above the waterline. Small icebergs, known as **growlers**, are difficult to detect on a ship's **sonar**.

Whale Alert!

Large humpback whales used to pose a danger to ships. They unwittingly could overturn a ship because of their sheer size. Today, ships are much bigger than whales, and the dangers are reversed. Large **tankers** and big **cargo ships** literally can run over whales while they lie sleeping in the water. Some enlightened companies now are developing electronic whale alarms to wake the whales so they have time to swim to safety.

Hurricanes

The **hurricane** season, between June and December, is particularly dangerous to ships in the Caribbean and Gulf of Mexico. There, the average sea temperature of 80 °F (27 °C) produces water vapor that rises and cools to form clouds. More warm air comes in from all sides to replace the rising air and creates an inward, circular wind that can reach 150 miles (240 km) per hour or more. The eye of the hurricane is a calm area in the center about 20 miles (32 km) in diameter.

Fog and Rocks

Ships have long relied on lighthouses to warn them of danger at sea, particularly around rocky coasts. The most famous lighthouse is the Pharos of Alexandria, one of the Seven Wonders of the Ancient World, which was built around 280 B.C. It now has vanished, but at the time, it was the tallest building on Earth, probably the height of a modern, 40-story building. The lighthouse had a mysterious mirror that could be seen 35 miles (56 km) from shore.

Storms

Bad storms at sea have been a common curse for sailors over the centuries. In the picture (*left*), the fishermen of a sinking **trawler** are being rescued in the storm-tossed North Sea.

In 1977, members of the Institute of Nautical Archaeology excavated the Serce Limani wreck, which was located 108 feet (33 m) underwater off the southern coast of Turkey. They found large amounts of broken glass littered around the site of the wreck. Divers mapped the area by creating a grid of the site with a square metal frame. They placed the frame over the remains, recorded the contents of the frame, and then moved the frame to a new part of the site. The location of every object was meticulously recorded. Gradually, **archaeologists** built a picture of a small two-masted ship with a Mediterranean sail, approximately 49 feet (15 m) long, dating from the eleventh century. It became clear that it was a cargo ship carrying goods for trade, including wine, raisins, bowls, and glassware. It also carried three tons of raw glass in small pieces that would have been used to manufacture glassware. It is likely that the ship was on its way to Constantinople (now Istanbul), the most important city at that time and a producer of Byzantine glassware.

The Site of the Wreck
The wreck was found in the harbor of Serce Limani on the southern coast of Turkey, opposite the Greek island of Rhodes.

Life in the Eleventh Century
The ship is a time capsule that helps historians understand life of the period. This filigree gold earring was probably used as a form of money, along with a few coins and other items of jewelry. Three lead seals used for documents were discovered among the remains. This suggests that the ship may have been carrying letters of credit rather than valuables that could be lost to pirates. Other items give a fascinating insight into eleventh-century life, such as the scissors, wooden comb, and chess set recovered from the living quarters.

The Restored Ship

The timbers of the wreck were brought to the surface and treated with polyethylene glycol, which preserves wood. The archaeologists then reassembled the pieces at the Bodrum Museum, specially built by the Turkish government. The ship was similar in construction to Egyptian vessels of the time, with a relatively flat bottom, steep sides, and hardly any **keel**, making it easy to navigate in shallow waters but unsuitable for open seas. The evidence of the retrieved timbers shows that the **shipwrights** had developed a method of covering a frame in order to build a hull instead of building the hull without a frame, which was common practice in the Mediterranean before the date of the wreck.

The Glass Jigsaw Puzzle

The archaeologists recovered hundreds of thousands of broken pieces of glass that they estimate once made up 10,000 to 20,000 glass objects. Two hundred of these objects, such as bottles and jugs, have been painstakingly pieced together in a giant glass jigsaw puzzle.

Underwater Archaeology

The glass goods, including jugs, jars, bottles, bowls, and cups, appear to have been made in Syria and look as if they were created in Islamic molds. The ship also was carrying glazed Islamic bowls, decorated with colored glazes, splashed on the inner surface, or with designs carved into the surface of the clay. Archaeologists also discovered 104 round clay pots with narrow necks. Most of the pots had been used for wine or olive oil.

The Mary Rose

One of the most famous shipwrecks is the *Mary Rose*, **flagship** of the **fleet** of King Henry VIII of England. The *Mary Rose* sank at Spithead off Portsmouth in 1545 with the loss of 500 lives. She carried a valuable supply of weapons, so people immediately attempted to **salvage** the ship. Efforts proved fruitless and were abandoned. In 1836, the Deane brothers discovered the wreck, using a diving helmet invented by John Deane. After the initial excitement, they also left the wreck alone. It was located once more in 1967, using modern sonar equipment. This time, a committee went to work to gain legal protection for the wreck, and in 1973, British Parliament passed the Protection of Wreck Act. In 1982, the *Mary Rose* Trust finally raised the wreck and established a museum in Portsmouth.

Down She Goes

While Henry VIII was at dinner on the flagship, five French galleys came into view in the Portsmouth harbor. Henry went ashore, and the *Mary Rose* led the fleet to engage the French. As Henry watched, horrified, from the nearby shore, the *Mary Rose*, pride of his fleet, sank. A survivor's report suggested that when she made a turn, water entered the lowest row of gun ports, which had stayed open after firing.

The brother of the Vice Admiral reported that she began to **heel** as soon as the sails were raised. When asked what was wrong, Vice Admiral Sir George Carew said that he had a hundred of the best sailors in the fleet, but that they quarrelled so much with one another out of pride and arrogance that they refused to take orders from one another. It seems the *Mary Rose* sank because of bad seamanship.

The Gravity of Guns

The *Mary Rose* had been remodeled in 1536, in the more modern "caravel" fashion with the planks laid directly adjacent to one another, instead of overlapping. This made it possible to cut square **gun ports** in the hull with efficient, watertight seals that could be lowered and tightly closed. The guns, therefore, could be put down in the hull, lowering the center of gravity and permitting two rows of gun ports instead of just one.

Henry VIII

Throughout Henry VIII's rule, he battled, on and off, with Francis I of France. The French, of course, tried to take credit for sinking the *Mary Rose*. Contemporary reports of the event differ. An engraving of the time shows that few ships had set sail, suggesting there was little wind, and that they were leaving Portsmouth at high water on an **ebb tide**. French reports stated that their **galleys** started battle at dawn on a calm sea, trying to lure the English toward their main fleet.

The *Mary Rose* Recovered

Engineers devised a plan to raise the ship from its resting place on the seabed by means of steel cradles that hoisted it to the surface. The wreck attracts thousands of visitors each year to its home in Portsmouth Dockyard.

BABCOCK POWER CONSTRUCTION DIVISION

All Human Life

The *Mary Rose* was a living picture of Tudor life when she sank. Archaeologists found a pewter jug, gold coins, musical instruments, and smooth, well-turned bowls on the wreck in the officers' quarters. They found a simple gaming board, roughly turned wooden tableware, nit combs, bows and arrows, crossbow bolts, sheathed knives, leather clothing, rope, barrels of tar, lanterns, firewood, and sailcloth in other parts of the ship. The crew appeared to be well nourished, perhaps because they fought only across narrow seas and always could get fresh supplies.

11

The Spanish Armada

By the mid-sixteenth century, Catholic Spain and France were both struggling for supremacy in Europe. In the 1580s, England's Protestant Queen, Elizabeth I, decided that the King of Spain's power should be curbed. In 1587, England directly challenged Spanish rule in the Netherlands. King Philip II of Spain prepared for battle. He warned his captains that the English had faster ships and would try to avoid fighting at close quarters because they had long-range guns. The Spanish **Armada** set sail from Lisbon in the early months of 1588 with 130 ships and more than 30,000 men ready to invade England. After a number of battles, the English sent **fireships** into the middle of the Armada as it lay anchored off Calais. This scattered the fleet and drove the Spanish north along the British coastline, where bad weather sank several ships. The Armada never recovered and decided to retreat to Spain.

Royal Rivals

Spain and England had formed a friendly alliance when Henry VIII's daughter, Mary I, married Philip II of Spain in 1554. After Mary's death in 1558, Philip felt it was his duty to protect English Catholicism despite his feeling that the English were difficult, ungrateful, and rebellious. Elizabeth I eventually claimed the English throne after Mary's death, and she set about embracing and extending the Protestant faith. By 1588, the two countries were set on a path to war, and Philip hatched a plan to invade England. He figured Spain would require an armada of naval ships to support the invasion.

A Treacherous Journey

This chart shows the track of the Armada around the British coastline. The Spanish encountered terrible weather, including freezing fog and storms. Between August 21 and September 3, seventeen ships disappeared during night storms as fierce winds drove the ships onto the Irish shore. The men who

were fortunate enough to reach dry land were captured and executed. The English considered the harsh treatment from the elements "divine retribution" against the Spanish. Clearly, God was on their side. As many as 11,000 **mariners** perished. Most of them drowned as their ships failed to withstand the pounding seas.

The Battle Rages

When the Spanish Armada came into view up the English Channel, the English fleet set sail from Plymouth, ready to engage in battle. Battles were fought off Plymouth, Portland, and the Isle of Wight.

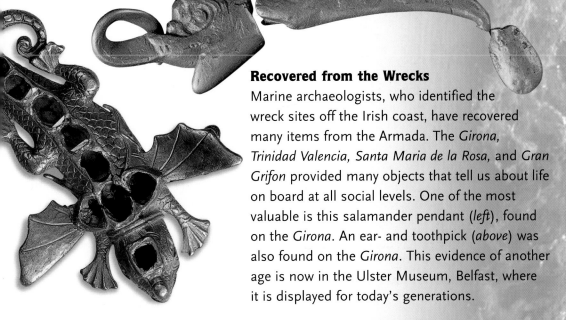

Recovered from the Wrecks

Marine archaeologists, who identified the wreck sites off the Irish coast, have recovered many items from the Armada. The *Girona*, *Trinidad Valencia*, *Santa Maria de la Rosa*, and *Gran Grifon* provided many objects that tell us about life on board at all social levels. One of the most valuable is this salamander pendant (*left*), found on the *Girona*. An ear- and toothpick (*above*) was also found on the *Girona*. This evidence of another age is now in the Ulster Museum, Belfast, where it is displayed for today's generations.

Spanish Gold

During the sixteenth and seventeenth centuries, European states expanded their empires overseas. In 1492, Christopher Columbus claimed the "New World" of the central Americas for Spain. These lands were known as the "Spanish Main," and the Spanish conquerers looted the rich treasures found there and shipped them back home. The richest **booty** came from the Aztecs of Mexico and the Incas of Peru, who had a great number of silver and gold items, many of them inlaid with precious stones. The Americas appeared enormously wealthy, and both the English and the French wanted to gain footholds. They resented the Spanish, who defended their monopoly fiercely. At first, the English and French commissioned **privateers** to attack the Spanish treasure ships, and many Spanish ships were sunk in the Caribbean. Francis Drake was one of the privateers. At first, he angered Elizabeth I, but then she backed him. Eventually, she made him a knight.

Atocha Treasure

Gold was a much-prized treasure. Francis Drake once plundered a mule train carrying 15 tons (15.24 metric tons) of gold — enough to build thirty Elizabethan warships. These **doubloons** (*left*) were recovered from the *Atocha*, a **galleon** lost near Cuba in a hurricane in 1622. She was loaded with gold and silver from Mexico. Many underwater treasure hunters dream of the glint of gold beneath the silt on the seafloor.

America

Columbus was the first European to set foot on the Spanish Main. In 1492, he was in pursuit of new trade routes and tried to find a sea passage to India and the East.

Spanish Silver

The Spanish systematically stripped the riches of countries like Bolivia and shipped them back to Spain. The native people were forced to work as slaves in mines such as the Cerro silver mine (*right*). The Europeans were ruthless masters.

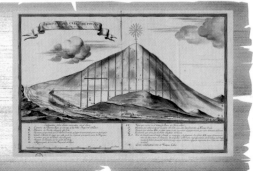

Warding off Rivals

Single ships or small squadrons of ships were easy prey for privateers, so, after 1543, the Spanish used two fleets to collect treasure from the Spanish Main. One fleet would collect Mexican treasure; the other, Peruvian gold and silver. About one hundred ships would then meet and sail back to Spain. The English attacked the ports that these treasure ships sailed from and tried to colonize them. In 1585, Drake led a fleet of twenty-one warships against Spanish-held Santo Domingo and Cartagena.

Spanish Galleon

Many Spanish ships, loaded with precious cargo, sank beneath the waves when they were attacked by pirates and privateers. Many probably still lie undiscovered on the seabed. For the few divers who have found such ships, the rewards are enormous because the gold, silver, and jewels have continued to accumulate value over the intervening centuries. The Caribbean Sea holds the secrets of many treasure ships, and the balmy, shallow waters are a perfect environment for amateur and professional divers alike.

Pirates!

Some Spanish soldiers joined up with groups of runaway slaves, deserters, and convicts, and together attacked the treasure ships for their own gains. These pirates lived by their own laws, and they were often ruthless and bloody. Sir Henry Morgan, who became governor of Jamaica, was probably the most famous **buccaneer,** and Blackbeard was the most famous pirate of all. By the mid-1700s, governments no longer turned to privateering. They established naval patrols in an effort to stamp out the pirate threat.

The Royal George

The *Royal George* sank on August 29, 1782, 1.5 miles (2.5 km) off Spithead near Portsmouth, in front of a fleet of thirty to forty ships. The weather was calm at the time. What makes this shipwreck notorious was that, of the twelve hundred people on board, nine hundred died, including Rear Admiral Richard Kempenfelt, head of the English fleet at that time. Three hundred women and sixty children were on board, and only one woman and one child survived. Witnesses said they heard a loud crack below deck. Others said they heard nothing. At the formal inquiry, Vice Admiral Mark Milbanke said that there was not a good piece of lumber in the ship, even though she had been **refitted** in 1782. The court martial decided that part of the frame gave out when she heeled (tilted), owing to the rotten state of her **timbers**. Some people felt this decision was a cover-up for the officers' incompetence and carelessness.

The *Royal George* at Dock

The *Royal George* was twenty-six years old, the oldest "first rate" ship in the service. On her last cruise, water started leaking into the *Royal George,* and the ship was ordered to dock. Experts surveyed her, found the leak, repaired it, and the ship avoided docking. On August 28, a deckhand noticed that the pipe delivering fresh water, which was situated just below the water line, was broken. The ship sank during the effort to repair this pipe.

Rum Made Them Tipsy

Admiral Kempenfelt gave the order to heel the *Royal George* so that the carpenter could reach the leaking freshwater pipe. Tons of **rum** barrels already kept the ship so low in the water that the slightest sea ripple entered the ship's lower gun ports. The order to heel brought the low side even lower, and the ship gradually began to fill with water and sink. Twice, the carpenter asked the lieutenant of the watch to right the ship. A sudden breeze blew, and water rushed in the lower ports. The workmen cried for the heeling to stop. The lieutenant gave the order, but too late. The ship went down, **starboard** side up. Although boats from the fleet came quickly to the scene, the whirlpool swirl of the sinking ship kept them away. On touching the seabed, she settled with her masts nearly upright.

Finding the *Royal George*

In July 1783, a man named Tracey tried to raise the *Royal George*. The British government supplied two ships and promised Tracey a large sum of money to do it. Tracey attached cables to the *Royal George*, making a cradle that moved it 30 feet (10 m), but bad weather created delays, and the race against the spring tides defeated him. He wanted to try again the next year but did not get permission.

Good Luck Lamb

The survivors included a plumber working below deck on a broken pipe and a seaman who was carried up the **hatchway** by water that rushed in. A young boy called Jack clung to a sheep and was rescued by a gentleman who later provided for him and called him Jack Lamb.

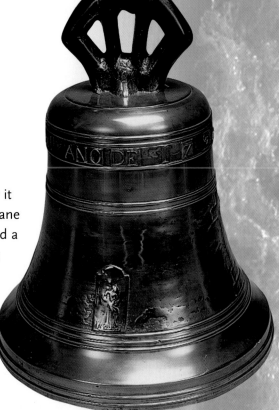

The *Royal George* Bell

In the nineteeth century, John Deane invented a copper-helmeted diving suit. He got the idea for it while trying to save some horses from a fire. Deane borrowed a helmet from a suit of armor, attached a long pipe to it, and went into a burning building while a farmer slowly pumped air through the pipe into the helmet. From 1834 to 1836, Deane and his brothers explored the wreck of the *Royal George*. Because their diving techniques were primitive, the most valuable items were salvaged first. These were the brass and iron guns and the ship's bell.

The *Medusa*

In 1816, a French frigate, *Medusa*, part of a squadron of four ships, set sail for Senegal in West Africa. The English were giving the colony of Senegal back to the French, so the *Medusa* was carrying many professional people for the diplomatic task ahead. The passengers and crews of the four ships consisted of an uneasy mix of Republicans and Monarchists. De Chaumarey, the captain of the *Medusa*, was in charge. He was a Monarchist who won his command as a favor from King Louis XVIII, even though he had not sailed for twenty-five years. At this time, the waters off the African coast were poorly charted, but the French Ministry warned de Chaumarey of the Arguin Bank, a particularly dangerous sandbank. They told him to steer well clear of it, although doing so would make the journey longer. During the voyage, the crew persuaded de Chaumarey to take the shortest and most dangerous route. By this time, the rest of the convoy had left the *Medusa*, following Ministry guidelines to take the safest route. On July 2, the *Medusa* ran aground on the sandbank. Confusion and indecision set in. The ship had only six **lifeboats**. Some suggested ferrying people ashore. Others said that if the ship were light enough, it could sail off the sand. One passenger suggested making a raft. The captain decided on the raft.

Napoleon Bonaparte

Emperor Napoleon was one of the most powerful leaders of history. His rule, however, saw terrible conflict between rival factions in his native France. It was his defeat at the Battle of Waterloo that ended French domination of Europe. England handed back Senegal as part of the peace settlement.

A Modern *Medusa*

A French film reenacting the events aboard the *Medusa* was as dramatic as the real event. The director tried to kill himself in front of the French Cultural Minister to draw attention to the fact that the film's release had been deliberately delayed.

Raft and Boats

The captain's plan was to build a raft that would carry 200 men, abandon the ship, and make for safety with the available boats. The ship's boats were supposed to tow the raft (see diagram *right*). After three days, the weather changed, and the *Medusa* started to break up, so the plan was put into action. De Chaumarey left with all the favored Monarchist passengers in the boats, along with their provisions. The raft, however, was badly constructed (*left*). It could carry only about 160 people, mainly soldiers, who were submerged up to their waists in water. Their only provisions were six barrels of wine and two barrels of water. This left sixty or so people, including women and children, who could not fit on the raft and were abandoned on the sinking *Medusa*.

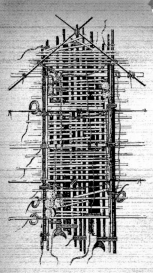

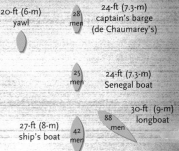

20-ft (6-m) yawl	28 men	24-ft (7.3-m) captain's barge (de Chaumarey's)
	25 men	24-ft (7.3-m) Senegal boat
27-ft (8-m) ship's boat	42 men	88 men	30-ft (9-m) longboat
	38 men	27-ft (8-m) governor's barge
	200 men	42 x 24 ft (12.8 x 7.3 m) raft

Cannibalism

Events on the raft quickly deteriorated. The men mutinied, and fighting broke out. Some were killed before they died from thirst and hunger. Some committed suicide. The survivors, forced by hunger, turned to cannibalism. Amazingly, after fifty-two days, the wreck finally was discovered with four men still alive. A total of 155 people died.

Raft of the Medusa

Theodore Géricault painted this masterpiece (*right*). He painted fifteen survivors and several trapped corpses afloat on the raft. Two of the survivors posed for the picture. It took ten months to do the first sketches and eight to make the painting. The painting originally had another title, "Scene of Shipwreck," perhaps because its true title was politically sensitive. There was still much bad feeling between the Monarchists and the Republicans.

The Titanic

Perhaps the most famous shipwreck of all time was the *Titanic*. The White Star Line announced that the *Titanic* and her sister ship, the *Olympic*, were the biggest, best, and safest passenger vessels afloat. It took 11,300 Harland & Wolff shipyard workers twenty-six months to build the *Titanic*. She was spacious, luxurious, supposedly unsinkable, and she had a service speed of 21 **knots** (24 miles/ 38 km per hour). The communication system was the most powerful ever used on a merchant vessel and, at night, had a range of 2,000 miles (3,218 km). The *Titanic* had a double-bottom construction and sixteen watertight compartments. Any two compartments could flood without affecting the buoyancy of the ship, thus assuring safety.

Leaving Southampton Harbor
The *Titanic* began her **maiden voyage** on April 10, 1912, sailing from Southampton to New York. Four days later, this magnificent ship was on the ocean floor.

The Sinking of the *Titanic*
On Sunday, April 14, 1912, traveling at approximately 20 knots (23 miles/38 km per hour), the *Titanic* hit an iceberg about 350 miles (563 km) southeast of Newfoundland. It was a dark night, with a slight mist and no moonlight. The ship had received several messages warning of **pack ice** and icebergs. A lookout saw the iceberg just before the ship hit. In trying to avoid a collision, the *Titanic* turned hard to starboard, but the iceberg hit it just below the waterline and ripped into the hull. The *Titanic* took two hours and forty minutes to sink. The ship's orchestra apparently continued to play until the final minutes.

The News Spreads

Only 705 people of the 2,228 on board survived. Those who made it into the lifeboats eventually were picked up by the *Carpathia*, which sailed as fast as she could to the scene of the wreck. She was too late, however, for those who did not find a lifeboat and quickly perished in the ice-cold water. Although distress calls were sent by wireless, by Morse lamp, and by rockets from the stricken ship, a ship said to be closer than the *Carpathia* never answered her calls. Some thought the mystery ship was the S.S. *Californian,* which had earlier sent an urgent ice warning to the *Titanic.* The *Titanic*'s wireless operator, busy with passenger telegrams, apparently told the *Californian*'s sender to "shut up." Later, he apologized and asked for the message to be repeated, but without success.

One of Many Tragic Tales

With 1,500 people left aboard and one lifeboat capable of carrying forty-seven people, the crew locked arms around the boat and told women and children to board. Michel Navratile, who had kidnapped his two sons from his wife, hoping to make a new start in the United States, handed the two boys over to the crew and told them to board the lifeboat. It was the last time the children saw their father.

Titanic Survivors

There were 2,228 people on board, but only enough lifeboats for 1,178. British safety regulations were based on cubic footage, not on the number of passengers. In fact, twenty lifeboats on board the *Titanic* exceeded government guidelines by 12 percent. The first lifeboats that left the ship, however, were not even full, such was the belief that the ship would never sink. The boats could have taken at least 53 percent of the people on board instead of the 32 percent who actually survived.

Remembering the Titanic

A British inquiry concluded that the iceberg damaged the bottom of the starboard side of the ship, about 10 feet (3 m) above the level of the keel, and that it took less than ten seconds to inflict 300 feet (100 m) of damage. As water filled the **bow** of the ship, the **stern** gradually rose out of the water. When the ship reached an angle of 60 degrees, it sank with lights still ablaze. Immediate plans were made to locate the wreck, but it lay 2.5 miles (4 km) beneath the surface, and technology at the time could not respond to the challenge. The *Titanic* then sank from public consciousness until 1958, when a British film company made *A Night to Remember*. In 1985, a joint French and American team discovered the *Titanic* by means of underwater video cameras. The ship lay in two pieces, ripped apart **amidships**. Exploration was difficult at such extreme depths, but the *Titanic's* mystery encouraged scientists to find new ways of visiting the wreck.

Truth in Art
As Jack Thayer watched the *Titanic* sink from one of the lifeboats, he drew the event unfolding before him. For many years, no one believed that his sketch of the hull breaking in two was accurate.

Exploring the *Titanic*

Nadir is the French government's undersea exploration ship. It worked with an American company, RMS *Titanic* Inc., to explore the wreck. *Nautile* is a three-man **submersible** with robotic arms that has been searching the wreck 19,600 feet (6,000 m) below the water surface and sending information back to *Nadir*. It takes one-and-one-half hours for *Nautile* to descend to the seabed. Because of the enormous pressure from the sea at this depth, *Nautile*'s core is made of titanium. Attached to *Nautile* is Robin, a video camera that can enter areas the submersible cannot penetrate.

Titanic — The Movie

In 1997, American film director James Cameron made a second film of the *Titanic* story. This epic film, centering on the fate of two star-crossed lovers who were passengers on the ship, proved to be one of the most successful films of all time. It broke box office records around the world. The special effects were based on evidence gathered from many dives to the shipwreck.

Titanic Model

This model of the *Titanic* shows the two main parts of the wrecked hull and how the ship lies on the seabed today.

May 7, 1915, was a warm spring day, and picnickers on the southern coast of Ireland watched in horror as a torpedo hit the starboard side of a British passenger ship, the *Lusitania*. A large explosion followed a few seconds later. In just eighteen minutes, the ship sank with the loss of 1,195 passengers and crew. Only 764 people survived. Of the dead, 123 were U.S. citizens. The disaster shocked the world. Surely no sailors of any civilized nation would sink an unarmed passenger liner! Survivors recall two explosions, yet records show that the German U-boat, *U-20*, fired only one torpedo. For years, there was speculation that the *Lusitania* was not an innocent passenger liner, as the British wanted everyone to believe. Some claimed she was carrying high explosives purchased in the United States for the British army to use in France. There was also a rumor that the British wanted the ship sunk so that the United States would join the Allied forces in the war against Germany.

Doomed

Launching the lifeboats was almost impossible. The crew was inexperienced, the passengers had no lifeboat drill, and the *Lusitania* was sinking fast. The ship leaned far over on its **port** (left) side. Most of the lifeboats had been smashed, and people on board tumbled into the sea. Only one or two boats made it into the water without damage.

True or False?

Photographs of victims and detailed sketches filled newspapers and magazines. Pictures such as this one (*above*), however, were not genuine. The clue that it was created for propaganda is that the name, *Lusitania,* in this picture is much too large.

The Propaganda War

The sinking of the *Lusitania* generated a great deal of publicity that the British government used as propaganda. Hundreds of posters and cartoons were produced that depicted the sinking ship, as well as press releases, photographs, scripts for slide shows, and articles for magazines. British military authorities noticed a strong increase in enlistments. It was a highly successful campaign and generated more support for the Allied cause than any number of political speeches.

LEST WE FORGET

The Sinking of the Lusitania.
May 7th 1915.

The Mass Funeral

Hundreds of bodies washed up on shore, days after the ship sank. Coffins in the Cunard yard held the dead while British soldiers dug mass graves in a cemetery outside Queenstown. Many passengers drowned because their life jackets were too loose or were upside down. Many more died because they did not have enough time to get to their life jackets. It was common practice in wartime for all crew and passengers to wear life jackets when they entered a danger zone, but the captain had not instructed them to do so. The inquests that followed failed to ask many relevant questions. The inquiry by the Board of Trade found Germany guilty and absolved the Cunard Line and the Royal Navy of blame.

Raising the *Lusitania*

In the 1930s, Jim Jarret was the first diver to stand on the wreck of the *Lusitania*. Wearing heavy, clumsy diving gear and looking at the ship in poor light, he thought the ship was lying on her port side. Twenty-five years later, with the aid of scuba gear and better lighting, John Light confirmed that the ship was, in fact, lying on her starboard side with a gigantic hole in the ship's port side. The fractured steel plate was bent outward, which he thought was a sure sign that there had been an internal explosion of tremendous force. This reinforced suspicions that the U-boat attack detonated illegal explosives.

One of the biggest news stories of 1956 was the sinking of the *Andrea Doria*. The Italian luxury liner was sailing toward New York on July 25, 1956, carrying 1,706 passengers and crew on her fifty-first transatlantic crossing. The liner was due in New York at 9 A.M. the next morning. She hit fog off the Nantucket coast. By evening, visibility was reduced to less than one-half mile (1 km). Under such conditions, the captain, Pietro Calamai, should have slowed the ship, but it appeared that he was anxious to make port on time. He reduced the ship's speed only a fraction from the maximum 23 knots (26 miles/42 km per hour). Also making its way through the fog that night, but outward bound from New York, was the *Stockholm,* a Swedish American passenger liner. The *Stockholm* carried 747 passengers and crew. The ships were headed for a fateful collision.

The Grande Dame of the Sea

The lavishly appointed *Andrea Doria* was thought to be unsinkable, just like the *Titanic* before her. It had been built to the latest safety standards just three years earlier.

Misreading

The ships were guided only by radar and had no radio communication. Apparently, they misinterpreted each other's courses. A formal inquiry faulted the fog, but it seems that mistaken radar procedures and following improper rules of the road were also to blame. The prow of the *Stockholm* hit the side of the *Andrea Doria* almost at a 90-degree angle. There was an immediate scramble for lifeboats as passengers attempted to save themselves. The *Stockholm* managed to secure watertight compartments and rescue passengers from the *Andrea Doria*. As the first news reporters arrived, flying over the scene to give eye-witness accounts of the ship's last moments, the *Andrea Doria* slowly slipped under the waves.

Collision Course

10:40 p.m.	The *Andrea Doria* picks up the *Stockholm* on its radar 17 miles (27 km) away.
10:50 p.m.	The *Stockholm* changes course.
11:05 p.m.	The *Andrea Doria* changes course. The ships are now closing in on each other.
11:07 p.m.	The *Stockholm* steers 20 degrees to starboard and the *Andrea Doria* takes emergency action, turning to port to avoid the other ship bearing down on her. The *Stockholm* turns to starboard in a final desperate avoiding action.
11:10 p.m.	The reinforced ice-breaking bow of the *Stockholm* plows into the starboard side of the *Andrea Doria*. The damage is severe.
11:20 p.m.	Captain Calamai sends the first S.O.S. message. He knows the *Andrea Doria* is doomed.
2:00 a.m	The liner *Ile de France* is the first ship to answer the S.O.S. and rescues 753 passengers.
5:30 a.m.	The captain and senior officers are the last to leave the stricken vessel.
10:09 a.m.	The *Andrea Doria* slips under the waves.

Admiral Doria

The *Andrea Doria* was named after the sixteenth-century Italian admiral depicted on this medal. His bronze statue adorned the first-class lounge and was the first artifact to be recovered by a salvage team in 1964.

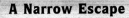

A Narrow Escape

Fourteen-year-old Linda Morgan had a narrow escape. She was thrown by the impact from cabin 52 on the *Andrea Doria* onto the deck of the *Stockholm*. She survived along with her mother, but her stepfather, Camille Cianfarra, foreign correspondent of the *New York Times*, was killed together with her eight-year-old stepsister. In all, fifty-one people died—forty-six on the *Andrea Doria* and five on the *Stockholm*. Many were killed by the impact when the bow of the *Stockholm* tore into cabins as passengers were preparing for bed.

Environmental Disasters

Modern shipwrecks can have a disastrous effect on the marine environment. Today's supertankers carry thousands of tons of crude oil, ready for refining into oil-based products such as gasoline. Today, the threats that sinking ships pose to human life are small compared to the harm the oil can do to the sea. Supertankers often carry only a handful of crew members, and safety at sea is much improved, thanks to accurate satellite navigation systems, the availability of detailed charts, and the sheer size of ships that can ride out rough weather. When something goes wrong, however, it does so on a huge scale, and human error is often to blame. Scientists have learned how to respond rapidly and effectively to disasters, such as oil spills, and are quick to minimize the damage that ensues.

The *Amoco Cadiz*

During a storm in 1978, the American supertanker *Amoco Cadiz*, filled with 223,000 tons of crude oil, ran aground off the Brittany coast of France and discharged its entire load into the Atlantic Ocean. About 130 beaches were coated in the oil, more than 30,000

seabirds died, and millions of crabs, lobsters, and other fish perished, which destroyed the livelihoods of many people. Standard Oil of Indiana was found guilty of negligence. It was cited for failure to train the ship's crew. In 1988, the Breton communities (some 400,000 people) affected by the disaster received $85 million in damages.

Sea Empress

The oil tanker *Sea Empress* ran aground in southwest Wales on February 5, 1996. Bad weather conditions made the ship's rescue extremely difficult, and the ship lost 72,000 tons of crude oil. Eventually the ship was towed to Belfast. The clean-up operation was put into effect very quickly.

The *Exxon Valdez*

In 1989, the *Exxon Valdez* ran aground at Prince William Sound in Alaska, dumping 267,000 barrels of oil (11 million gallons/41,640 liters) over almost 10,000 square miles (25,900 sq km). Its effect on the ecosystem was severe and made more so because the accident happened in cold water. This prolongs the life of toxins and affects wildlife species for generations. At the time, it was the largest oil spill ever in the United States.

Wildlife in Danger

In the *Exxon Valdez* disaster, thousands of seabirds, otters, fish, and kelp were killed as well as 16 whales and 147 bald eagles.

Clean-up

The clean-up operation after the *Exxon Valdez* disaster has been heavily criticized for its mismanagement. Damaging hydrocarbons were permitted to seep into the earth. Clean-up after the *Sea Empress* disaster was one of the most successful because many lessons were learned from earlier oil spills. Workers recovered oil from the sea in sheltered areas and broke it down with chemicals. They treated the oil that coated the beaches with high pressure hoses and scrapers. For rocky areas, they used absorbent materials to soak up the oil. Inaccessible areas were left to the natural cleaning power of the sea.

Human Disasters

Tragedies at sea that result in terrible loss of life are still commonplace despite the advances in ship technology and safety measures. Often, human error is to blame. Crew negligence or passenger ignorance can result in disaster. Ferries, which operate — and often sink — in shallow coastal waters, have lost large numbers of people. Some disasters have occured in inland waters, such as the ferry *MV Bukoba*, which sank in Lake Victoria, Tanzania, in 1996 with huge loss of life. The ferry was badly overcrowded, which may have been a factor in its capsizing. The following year, about 180 passengers drowned when a Haitian ferry sank just a few hundred yards from shore. In October, 2003, the Staten Island Ferry in New York crashed into a pier, killing ten people and sending thirty-four to the hospital.

Greenpeace Sinking

The environmental pressure group Greenpeace purchased the trawler *Sir William Hardy* for its campaign to protect whales in the North Atlantic. Renamed *Rainbow Warrior*, she was painted in rainbow colors. A dove of peace carrying an olive branch adorned the bow. Greenpeace used her in many protests against activities that posed a threat to the environment. In 1985, the *Rainbow Warrior* arrived in New Zealand to protest French nuclear testing in French Polynesia. While she was in the harbor, French secret agents bombed the vessel and sank it. A Greenpeace photographer drowned trying to retrieve his equipment. After two years of arbitration, the French government paid Greenpeace $8.159 million in compensation.

A Fishy Home

The *Rainbow Warrior* was buried at sea in Matauri Bay in New Zealand with a full Maori ceremony on December 12, 1987. The wreck, sunk in deep, clear waters, has become an artificial reef with an abundance of life. Many divers visit it. In 1989, Greenpeace launched a new *Rainbow Warrior*, another North Sea trawler, that includes an educational theater and workshop.

The *Herald of Free Enterprise*

On March 6, 1987, a car ferry, the *Herald of Free Enterprise*, left a harbor in Belgium with 500 passengers and 80 crew. Twenty minutes into the journey and 1.5 miles (2.5 km) from shore, the vessel capsized in freezing cold water. It took just sixty seconds to turn over. Eleven hundred tons of cars and trucks shifted to one side along with the passengers and anything that wasn't fastened down. There wasn't even time for a Mayday call. Nearly 200 lives were lost. A dredger saw the ship capsize and immediately raised the alarm. Within thirty minutes, salvage ships, tugs, and a helicopter were on the scene.

The *Herald of Free Enterprise* Rescue Operation

This rescue operation was well organized and efficient. Within fifteen minutes, specialist teams were ready in hospitals. Later, the *Herald of Free Enterprise* was successfully raised to determine the cause of the disaster. Investigators found that the doors of the car deck had been left open, which allowed water to rush onto the lower deck, destabilizing the vessel.

The *Estonia* Ferry Disaster

On September 27, 1994, the ferry *Estonia* sailed from Estonia to Stockholm carrying 989 passengers. About halfway across the Baltic Sea and in heavy seas with 20-foot (6-m) waves, the ferry's huge steel bow door was torn from its hinges by the force of the sea.

The ship listed to one side, allowing seawater to pour into the lower decks. The crew, unsure of what happened, maneuvered the *Estonia* sideways, hoping the wind and waves would push her back onto an even keel. It had the opposite effect. Twenty tons of water entered the stricken vessel per second. The photograph (*left*) shows the bow door that was later recovered.

The *Estonia*'s Life Rafts

Passengers of the *Estonia* struggled to get to the open decks as the ship rolled over. They scrambled onto the upturned hull, but the waves washed them off. Within fifty minutes, the ship sank. Only 137 passengers survived. Many were trapped and never made it into the forty life rafts that floated, mostly empty, on the freezing seas.

31

Gazetteer

Thousands of wrecked ships litter the world's oceans. Even today, the fishing fleets of every nation regularly lose ships at sea, but these daily tragedies never make it into news headlines. Most of the ships that founder at sea never will be discovered, and the causes never will be known. The relentless movement of the waves and the corrosive power of salt water quickly reduce sunken ships until nothing recognizable remains. Occasionally, divers discover wrecks and retrieve a little piece of history before it is consumed forever beneath the waves. This map shows the locations of the wrecks described in this book.

North America

Pacific Ocean

N

South America

The *Exxon Valdez*
The *Exxon Valdez* ran aground in Alaska.

The *Andrea Doria*
The ship was named after the sixteenth-century Italian Admiral depicted on this medal.

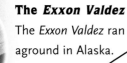

The *Medusa*
Theodore Géricault's masterpiece, "Raft of the *Medusa*," created waves.

Treasure
Doubloons were recovered from the *Atocha*.

The *Titanic*
The *Titanic* sank on her maiden voyage.

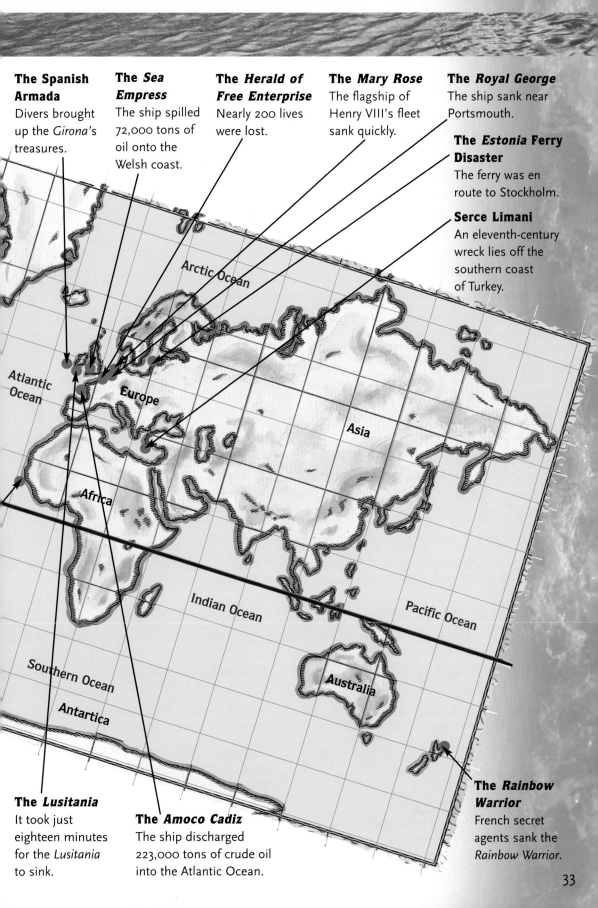

The Spanish Armada
Divers brought up the *Girona's* treasures.

The *Sea Empress*
The ship spilled 72,000 tons of oil onto the Welsh coast.

The *Herald of Free Enterprise*
Nearly 200 lives were lost.

The *Mary Rose*
The flagship of Henry VIII's fleet sank quickly.

The *Royal George*
The ship sank near Portsmouth.

The *Estonia* Ferry Disaster
The ferry was en route to Stockholm.

Serce Limani
An eleventh-century wreck lies off the southern coast of Turkey.

Arctic Ocean

Atlantic Ocean

Europe

Asia

Africa

Indian Ocean

Pacific Ocean

Southern Ocean

Australia

Antartica

The *Lusitania*
It took just eighteen minutes for the *Lusitania* to sink.

The *Amoco Cadiz*
The ship discharged 223,000 tons of crude oil into the Atlantic Ocean.

The *Rainbow Warrior*
French secret agents sank the *Rainbow Warrior*.

33

Stories of Survival

The Wedding

The Indonesian ferry *Gurita* sank in a storm off the coast of Malaysia in January 1996. More than 150 people were lost, but among the forty-seven survivors were Londoner Steve Nicholson and his girlfriend Caroline Harrison. Harrison overcame her fear of the sea to take the ferry that night but was plunged into the sea as the ferry sank. Together, they kept afloat for more than twelve hours. Not knowing whether they would survive, Steve proposed marriage, and Caroline accepted.

Shark Alert

New Yorker Margaret Crotty was also a passenger on the *Gurita*. When the ferry sank, Crotty jumped into the sea. She grabbed hold of a rubber life raft but was pushed off by passengers who feared it might capsize. Crotty removed her

trousers, knotted the legs and trapped air into them, creating a balloon that helped her stay afloat for sixteen hours before she finally reached land. She had cut her leg getting off the ferry, and her greatest fear was that hungry sharks might be attracted by the blood.

Saved by a Bucket

In 1993, the ferry *Neptune* sank in a storm off the coast of Haiti. About two thousand passengers were on board, but only 285 survived. The captain, Benjamin St. Clair, said the passengers panicked when the ferry began to roll in the heavy seas. They rushed from one side to the other. One survivor hugged a bag of charcoal for fifteen hours after being swept into the sea. One woman survived by hanging onto a small white bucket. The ship carried no lifeboats, life jackets, radios, or other emergency equipment.

Web Sites

Shipwreck Island Adventure!

oncampus.richmond.edu/academics/ education/projects/webquests/shipwreck/
Travel to exotic islands in pursuit of a mysterious message in a bottle on a web adventure. Locate an ancient sunken ship.

Shipwreck Central

www.shipwreckcentral.com
The largest collection of shipwreck videos on the web. The interactive map holds hundreds of wrecks waiting to be explored.

Shipwrecks Magazine

www.geocities.com/shipwrecks_magazine
Sample pages from the printed quarterly magazine.

Wisconsin's Great Lakes Shipwrecks

www.wisconsinshipwrecks.org
Photos and video of Lake Michigan and Lake Superior wrecks, diving history, and information on local underwater archaeology and research.

Glossary

amidships — midway between bow and stern

apparatus — equipment designed for a particular use

aqualung — a diving apparatus that automatically provides air to divers from bottles strapped on their backs

archaeologists — people who study objects from past human life and activities

armada — a fleet of warships

atmospheric diving suit — an armored, jointed diving suit that protects the diver from water pressure at great depths

booty — plunder taken on land as distinguished from prizes taken at sea

bow — the forward part of a ship, the prow

buccaneer — any of the freebooters preying on Spanish ships in the seventeenth century

cargo ships — ships that carry goods or freight

doubloons — old Spanish coins

ebb tide — the receding tide that flows out to sea

fireships — ships carrying combustibles or explosives sent burning among the enemy's ships

flagship — a ship that carries the commander of the fleet and flies the commander's flag

fleet — a number of warships under a single command

galleon — a heavy, square-rigged sailing ship of the fifteenth to early eighteenth century used for war or commerce

galleys — long, low ships used for war

global positioning system (GPS) — a navigational system using satellite signals to fix the location of a radio receiver

growlers — small icebergs, less than 3 feet (1 m) tall

gun port — an opening through which guns may be fired

hatchway — a passage giving access to an enclosed space

heel — to tip or lean to one side

hull — the frame or body of a ship exclusive of the masts, yards, sails, or rigging

hurricane — a tropical cyclone with winds of 74 miles (119 km) per hour or greater, usually accompanied by rain, thunder, and lightning

keel — the part of a boat that projects vertically from the bottom in the center of the boat

knot — one nautical mile per hour

lifeboats — sturdy boats used for emergencies at sea

maiden voyage — a ship's first trip across the sea

mariners — sailors

pack ice — sea ice packed together into a mass

port — the left side of a ship, facing forward

privateers — armed private ships licensed to attack enemy shipping

reefs — ridges of rock, sand, or coral

refitted — repaired, renovated, or resupplied

rum — an alcoholic beverage

salvage — to save or rescue a ship or its cargo

shipwrights — shipbuilders

sonar — device for locating objects, especially underwater, by means of sound waves

starboard — the right side of a ship looking forward

stern — the rear of a ship

submersible — a small, underwater craft used for deep-sea exploration

tankers — cargo ships with tanks for carrying liquid in bulk

timbers — the lumber or boards used to build a ship

time capsules — containers holding historical records or objects representative of the time for preservation until some future age

trawler — fishing boat

vessels — watercraft bigger than a row boat

wet suit — close-fitting suit made of a material that traps a thin layer of water against the body to retain body heat

Index